Needle Crafts 16

CROCHET

SEARCH PRESS
Tunbridge Wells

INTRODUCTION

Crochet is a simple handicraft. All you do is to collect a thread in the hook head and pull it through the loop already on the hook to form a chain. Should you drop a stitch, only one single knot is undone.

The very simplicity of crochet enables it to be extremely versatile. Different textures can be produced by using a variety of yarns or by altering the point of insertion of the hook into the work. Crochet can be worked in any direction to give both flat and 3–dimensional effects. Shaping is included as the work progresses, new colours may be introduced with ease and edges can be decoratively finished.

This book explains the working of basic stitches and common processes, with diagrams and patterns.

MATERIALS AND EQUIPMENT

Yarns

The range and textures of yarns available has never been more varied nor their fibre content so mixed. This, plus the enormous range of colour, makes the business of choosing yarn exciting. The crochet hook is particularly suitable for coping with textured yarns of any thickness as the work is less sensitive to thin and thick patches within the yarn than, for example, knitting.

Amounts

Buy enough yarn to complete your project, and check that colours come from the same dye batch. Yarns are now bought by the gramme. For old patterns, the equivalent in ounces is as follows:
8 oz yarn equals 9 balls @ 25g or 12 balls @ 20g.
16 oz yarn equals 9 balls @ 50g or 12 balls @ 40g or 18 balls @ 25g or 23 balls @ 20g.

Hooks

A crochet hook is a rod of metal, plastic, bone or wood with one end shaped into a hook. The centre is often flattened to enable it to be held by the fingers. A good hook is strong and smooth. Prior to metrifi-cation, hooks in Britain were numbered, the higher the number the finer the hook; and they were of two kinds: the hook for wool was made of plastic, bone or occasionally wood, and the hook for cotton was made of metal.

Since metrification only the smallest hooks are made in metal, or have metal tips with plastic handles. They are now numbered in metric units, the higher the number the larger the hook. However, there are still many useful old patterns and old hooks around. The chart on page 30 compares metric sizes, English wool and cotton sizes, and the American equivalents.

Other equipment

You will also need a pair of sharp scissors; a tape measure marked in centimetres and inches; a large blunt tapestry needle; and safety pins.

METHOD OF WORK

The basic processes are described in the following pages. If you are left-handed, read the diagrams by placing them at an angle in front of a mirror, and transpose the words 'left' and 'right' in the text.

Holding the hook

Hold the crochet hook gently as you would a pen, between the thumb and first finger and resting against the middle finger.

The hook should be turned towards you.

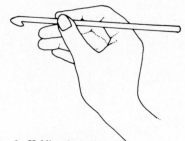

Fig 1 Holding the hook

Holding the yarn

The left hand holds the work and feeds in the yarn from the ball, regulating the tension. Take the yarn round the third and little finger, and bring it over the middle finger. The work is held between the index finger and the thumb, leaving a gap between the middle and index fingers in which to insert the hook.

Fig 2   Holding the yarn

STARTING WORK

No crochet can be worked unless there is a loop on the hook.

This is achieved by making a slip knot. Because all stitch processes start and end with one loop, at no time is this loop counted as a stitch.

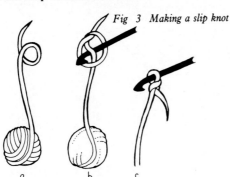

Fig 3   Making a slip knot

a   b   c.

Making a slip knot

a) Make a circle with the yarn.
b) Keep the ball thread behind, insert the hook from right to left and pull it through.
c) Tighten the loop.

BASIC STITCHES

All crochet stitches stem from variations of a chain, double crochet or treble. Stitches have different names in different countries, so check the source of your pattern. The terms used throughout this book are English. You could work small samples of stitches, to be kept for reference, or join them together to make a small knee rug, tote bag, or cushion cover.

Chain (ch)

Hold the slip knot in the left hand between finger and thumb. *Place hook under yarn from right to left (yarn round hook, or yrh, as in Fig 4). Draw yarn through the loop already on the hook one chain stitch made (ch). Repeat from * for the required length. Chain is the foundation stitch of crochet and usually forms the base of the first row or round.
1 To count the chains, *do not* count the loop on the hook but begin counting as in Fig 4.

page 4:
Belt *made of decorated wood crocheted together with a linen yarn. Inspiration for the design came from the painted leather garments of North American Indians.*
(Pauline Turner)

page 5:
Tree Panel – *Worked in chain stitch on threads stretched across a wire ring. The basic chain is looped to produce a foliar effect. The idea was derived from a creative class given by Sylvia Cosh.*
(Anne Smith)

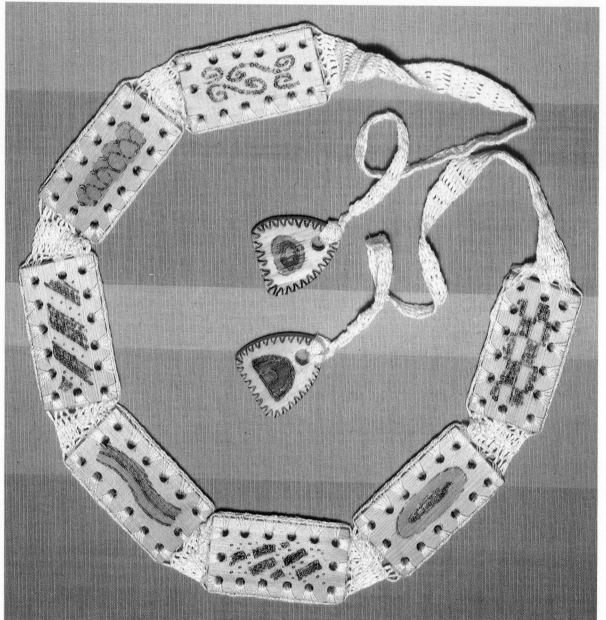

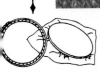

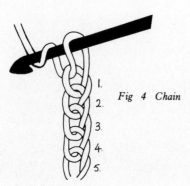

Fig 4 Chain

2. When working a stitch into the foundation chain, insert the hook under the top two threads (Fig 5) to give a neat 'buttonhole' look to the base edge.

3. Make as many chains in your foundation chain as the number of stitches required, plus turning chains.

The turning chain

The first row of stitches is made by working back along the foundation chain and making one stitch in each chain. Unlike knitting, where every stitch is the same size, crochet stitches vary in height so that every new row must begin with a number of chains to lift the hook up to the required position. The number of turning chains depends on the kind of stitch you will make.

When you reach the end of the row, you will also work into the turning chain which you made at the beginning of the previous row (Fig 11b).

Turning chains count as the first stitch of the row, so (with the exception of half trebles) *miss the space directly beneath them* and work into the next stitch. See Fig 11a.

The following list shows the number of turning chains needed to lift the hook to the correct position.

slip stitch	–	none
double crochet	–	one chain
half treble	–	two chains
treble	–	three chains

The right side

Unless texture or a shaping is included in the work, there is no right side to crochet. If a right side is indicated in the pattern, place a marker of contrasting thread to show which is the right side.

Hook insertion

Always insert the hook under the top two horizontal threads unless the pattern indicates otherwise. Inserting the hook in a different way will alter the texture and sometimes the tension.

Learn the movements and see what a section of each stitch looks like. Practise with different sizes of hook and types of yarn, thereby learning also about tension and texture.

Double crochet (dc) (1 turning chain)

Double crochet is the smallest stitch in crochet, and results in a close firm fabric showing a small pattern.

Place hook into work, yarn round hook (yrh), draw yarn through to the front (two loops on hook). Yrh and draw through these two loops.

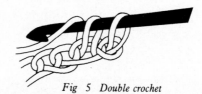

Fig 5 Double crochet

To work a square of double crochet

1. Work a row of 10 chain.
2. Work 1 extra (turning) chain.
3. Start next row by inserting the hook, from front to back, under the top two horizontal threads of the third chain from the hook.
4. Wrap yarn round hook (yrh) and draw it to the front (two loops on the hook).
5. Yrh again, then draw the yarn through both loops on the hook – result, one double crochet made.

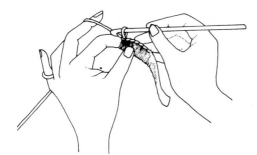

Fig 6a End of a row

Fig 6b Turning work, starting next row

6. Insert the hook into each chain in turn, and make a double crochet by repeating steps 4 and 5.

7. At the end of the row, turn the work as shown in Figs 6a and 6b, by keeping the hook and loop in the right hand, and turning the crochet over from right to left.

8. Work one turning chain (which counts as the first stitch of the next row).

9. Miss the last stitch of the previous row and work a double crochet into the next stitch.

10. At the end of the row, work the last double crochet into the turning chain of the previous row.

11. Work one turning chain, turn the work, and work another row of double crochet.

12. Continue until the square is complete.

Half treble (htr) (2 turning chains)

Wrap yarn round hook before inserting it under top two threads of next stitch. Yrh, draw yarn to front of work (three loops on hook). Yrh again (Fig 7), draw through all three loops. 1 htr made.

Fig 7 Half treble

Treble (tr) (3 turning chains)

The most common stitch in crochet is treble. Double crochet is a short stitch producing a dense fabric. A treble fabric is quicker to make, and the stitch is capable of more variations. Wrap yarn round hook. Insert hook under top two threads of next stitch. Yrh, draw through to front of work (three loops on hook). Yrh and draw through first two loops (Fig 8), yrh and pull through remaining two loops. I tr made.

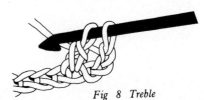

Fig 8 Treble

page 8:
Tailored Jacket – *Beige double knitting wool and camel coating material. Treble clusters and dc form the main part of the crochet. The cuffs are made in trebles that have been worked round the stems of the rows below to give a ridged effect.* (**Ena Garside**)

page 9:
Denim Jacket – *Some of the pattern pieces are replaced with crocheted cotton mesh. This is a simple crocheted net of 1 tr 2 ch with occasional blocks of 3 trs.*
(**Pauline Turner**)

Double treble (dtr) (4 turning chains)

Wrap yarn twice round hook before inserting into work. Yrh, draw through to front of work (four loops on hook) – (Fig 9). **Yrh and draw through first two loops on hook. Repeat from ** twice. 1 dtr made.

Fig 9 Double treble

Slip Stitch (ss) (no turning chain)

Insert hook into the work under two threads, yrh and pull through all loops now on hook. The slip stitch is used for joining rounds or carrying the yarn across stitches as it has no height.

Fig 10 Slip stitch

SHAPING

Rectangles (with straight sides worked in trebles)

Any basic stitch can be worked in rows to form a fabric. The method with which to ensure even straight sides is to work the turning chain at the beginning of a row, but note that this stands as the first stitch. Insert the hook in the next stitch, missing the top of the stitch immediately at the base of the turning chain (Fig 11a).

Fig 11a Turning chain and starting the row. Insert hook under top two threads

Proceed along the row making one stitch for every stitch of the row below. The hook should be inserted under the top two threads of each stitch until you reach the end. The last stitch is worked into the top of the turning chain of the row below (Fig 11b).

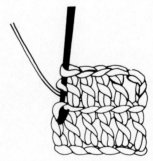

Fig 11b Ending the row. Insert hook in top of turning chain

Triangle (increasing)

Triangle, worked in trebles.

To increase, put two stitches where normally there would be one. To practise this make a triangle of trebles. Commence with 4 ch and in the first chain made (*ie* 4th ch from hook) work 2 trebles – 3 stitches in all. Next row: 3 ch, 1 tr in the same place as turning ch (see Fig 12), 1 tr, 2 tr in last st.

Continue putting 2 stitches in the first and last one of every row until the triangle is the size required.

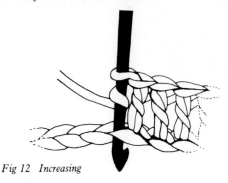

Fig 12 Increasing

Diamond (increasing and decreasing)

Diamond, worked in trebles.

To practise decreasing, first work a triangle as shown above until the diamond is as wide as required. Now decrease 1 st at the beginning and end of every row until all the stitches have been worked off.

To decrease without leaving holes or having irregular sides work as follows:– make the turning chain, work the next stitch until there are two loops left on

page 12:
Jacket in two colours *with a crab stitch edge, fringing and covered toggles.* (**Pauline Turner**)

page 13:
Overtop *using many yarns of different thicknesses and texture. This was designed to show how easy it is to mix stitches, textures, fibre content etc.*
(**Olive Gordon**)

Fig 13 Decreasing

the hook; work the next stitch until there are 3 loops left (*ie* the original loop, one loop from the first stitch of decrease, one loop from the second stitch of decrease); yrh and draw through all 3 loops – decrease of one stitch made. To decrease by one stitch at the end of a row, work along the row to the last 2 stitches and decrease one stitch as above (Fig 13).

'T' – Shape

To increase a large number of stitches work a chain equal to the number of stitches required plus the correct number of turning chain. If the increasing is to take place at both sides of the work, use another ball to add the correct number of chain at the opposite end and then break off this extra yarn (Fig 14). Now proceed along the two extensions and the body of the work in the normal way.

Fig 14 Increasing for a 'T' shape

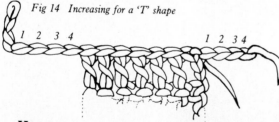

Hexagon

Crochet can be worked in rounds. Start with 4 ch and join with a slip stitch. Into the hole (made by the chain ring) work 1 ch to raise the hook, and 5 dc, join this round with a ss (6 sts in all). To keep the hexagon flat it is necessary to increase on every row by 6 dc, therefore the second round has to have 2 sts

in every st making 12 sts: the third round requires 2 sts in *every other* stitch. Continue increasing at the *same points* on every round.

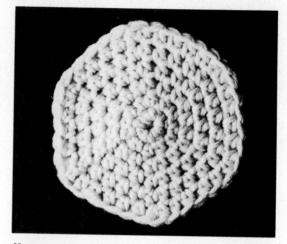

Hexagon, worked in double crochet.

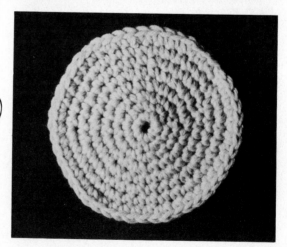

Circle, worked in double crochet.

Circle

A true circle of dc is made in the same way as the hexagon but working the 6 increases per round in different places.

As the circumference of the circle gets bigger, continue to work the same number of increases per round to keep the shape flat.

SYMBOLS

As a shorthand method of writing patterns, stitches and instructions can be represented by symbols. A list of these will be found on page 31. Shapes like the ones shown here can be expressed in symbolic diagrams.

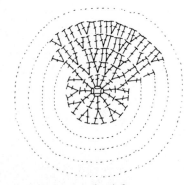

Fig 15   Symbolic diagram of a circle

To make a circle in trebles put 12 sts in all, in the centre of the 4 ch ring and increase by 12 sts on every round, once more remembering to stagger the points of increase.

Octagon

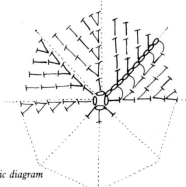

Fig 16   Symbolic diagram of an octagon

To make an octagon in half treble place 8 sts in the centre of the 4 ch ring (2 turning ch and 7 htr). Then increase in the same place on every round by 8 sts.

Cup-shape

Circles can be transformed into cup-shapes by putting less increases per round than is necessary for a circle, *eg* increase by 6 sts per round in a circle of trebles instead of 12. To build up the sides of the cup you may not need to increase at all.

Clusters (cl)

The term 'cluster' is given to a group of stitches which have been drawn together at the top. It does not matter if the base of the group of stitches is worked in the same place or fanned out and worked in consecutive stitches. The photograph of the decorative circle shows how the clusters on Row 3 have been worked into a single stitch.

page 16:
Stalactite Cave No II *Three-dimensional knitted and crocheted soft sculpture, using a very wide variety of yarns in a limited range of colours.* (**Jan Messent**)

page 17:
The Circular Shawl *is 56" in diameter and worked in 2-ply wool using mainly trebles on a large hook. The knitted wedding ring shawls of Northern Scotland acted as the catalyst for the design.* (**Pauline Turner**)

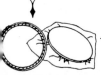

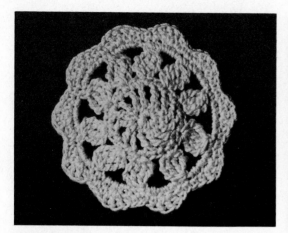

A decorative circle.

Rose motif with four layers of petals.

Pattern for a decorative circle (above)

4 ch, join into a ring with a ss.

1. 2 ch, work 11 dc into the centre of the ring, join to second of 2 ch with a ss.

2. 5 ch *1 dtr (Fig 9) 1 ch, rep from * 10 times, join into 4th ch of the 5 ch at beg. of row with a ss (12 sts).

3. 4 ch, 3 dtr worked into the same place as ss but leaving the last loop of each st on the hook, yrh draw through the 4 loops, 4 ch, miss 1 st, * 4 dtr cluster in next st, 4 ch, miss 2 sts, rep from * 8 times, 4 ch, miss 1 st, join into top of first cluster with a ss.

4. 1 ch, * 1 dc 1 htr 1tr 1 dtr 1 tr 1htr 1 dc into 4 ch loop, rep from * 9 times, join with ss.

Rose motifs

A rose motif, whether incorporated in the old trad-itional Irish crochet or used in a modern manner, consists of rounds of petals which are allowed to remain raised and free from the base fabric. Only the last round is anchored into surrounding work. The number of petals is a matter of personal choice.

The instructions following are for a typical Irish rose motif of only two rounds of petals.

Pattern for rose motif

5 ch joined with ss.

Rnd 1: 1 ch, 11 dc in centre of ring.

Rnd 2: 5 ch, miss 1 dc ** 1 dc in next dc, 4 ch, miss 1 dc, 1 dc in next dc, rep from ** 4 times, 4 ch, miss 1 dc, join with ss into first of 5 ch.

Rnd 3: In each ch sp work 1 dc 1 htr 3 tr 1 htr 1 dc to form a petal. Join with ss to first dc.

Rnd 4: Working behind petals just made ss into back of dc of rnd 2 ** 5ch, ss into next dc of rnd 2 rep from ** 5 times.

Rnd 5: In each ch sp work 1 dc 1 htr 5 tr 1 htr 1 dc. Join with ss.

Rnd 6: Working behind petals ** ss into ss of rnd 4 3816 ch rep from ** 5 times ss into ss of rnd 4.

Rnd 7: Into each ch sp work 1 dc 1 htr 1 tr 3 dtr 1 tr 1 htr 1 dc. Join with ss. Break off yarn.

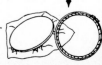

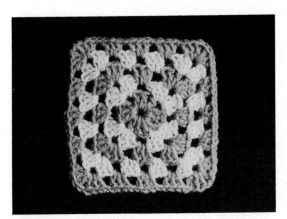

A 'Granny' square.

Squares

Squares can be made from circles by increasing only at the 4 corners. For the 'Granny' square the principle of increasing 12 trebles per round is the same as for the treble circle, with the difference that at the same 4 points, 3 extra stitches are inserted on every round. When the same number of stitches are grouped together at intervals within a pattern the publishers will frequently refer to them as either groups or blocks thus reducing the amount of print otherwise required.

A group or block refers to complete stitches unlike a cluster.

The following is the symbolic instruction for a granny square.

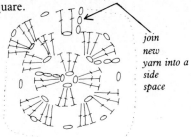

join new yarn into a side space

Fig 17 Symbolic diagram of a 'Granny' square

Pattern for a 'Granny' square using two colours - (also known as Afghan square)

In main colour.
4 ch, join into a ring with a ss.
3 ch 2 tr into ring ** 1 ch 3 tr, rep from ** twice, 1 ch join to 3rd of 4 ch at beginning of row with ss. Break off yarn.
Round 2: Attach contrast to any ch sp.
3 ch 2 tr 1 ch 3 tr 1 ch in that space, ** 3 tr 1 ch 3 tr 1 ch in next space, repeat from ** twice, join to 3rd of 3 ch with ss. Break off yarn.
Round 3: Attach main colour to any side space, ie any space between groups (or blocks) (Fig 16) 3 ch 2 tr 1 ch, ** 3 tr 1 ch 3 tr in next space, 1 ch 3 tr in next sp 1 ch rep from ** twice, 1 ch 3tr in next sp, 1 ch, join with ss. Break off yarn.

A granny square can be enlarged to any size by working 1 group of 3 trebles in the side spaces and 2 groups of 3 trebles in the corner spaces. Separate all groups of trebles with a chain and join all rounds with a ss.

EDGINGS

Crab Stitch – also known as Russian stitch, corded edge, rope edge (or stitch), shrimp stitch and reversed double crochet – This gives a tailored look to crochet and removes the 'chain stitch' edge. With right side (rs) of work facing do a double crochet from left to right instead of right to left. Check there are two loops on hook when collecting yarn to the front, otherwise a backward slip stitch will be the result. (Fig 19).

Fig 18 Crab stitch

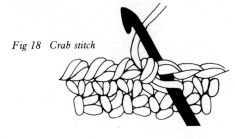

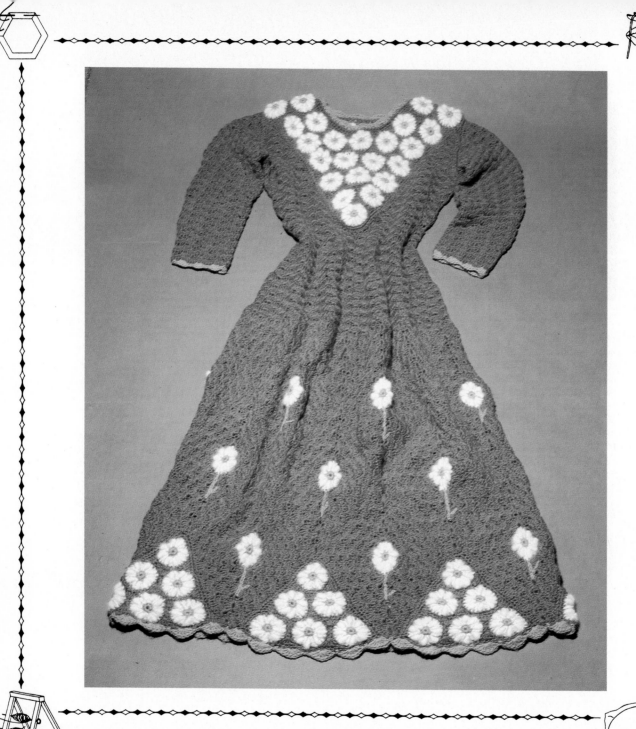

Shell edge

A shell gives a scallop edge and is useful for some knitwear, baby clothes, bedjackets and lacy tops or evening wear.

With RS facing 1 ss ** miss 2 sts, 5 tr in next st, miss 2 sts, 1 ss. Rep from ** to end.

Picot edge

This attractive finish to a garment has the same uses as a shell edge but is neater and smaller adding very little length to the article.

With RS facing, 4 ch, 1 ss into 3 ch from hook, ** miss 1 st, 1 dc 3 ch 1 ss into first ch made. Rep from ** to last st, 1 dc. Break off yarn.

INSERTIONS/SUBSTITUTIONS

Crochet is particularly attractive when inserted into a garment. Try the following design making the strips of crochet as long as required. Remember to reduce the fabric of the article to compensate for the width of the crochet insertion to ensure a good fit.

1. Embroider a length of chain stitch along folds of the fabric made by pressing back the two sides of the seam allowance of the article.
2. Crochet 1 dc into each embroidered chain on one piece of the fabric. If the work is puckering, change the crochet to 1 dc 1 ch for each embroidered ch.

page 20:
Evening Dress *using double knitting wool and shells of treble for its base. The flower motifs have dc centres in green and petals of mohair worked in boullion stitch (wrap yarn 10 times round hook, insert into st, yrh and draw through to the front, yrh, and pull through all 12 loops at once). The design was taken from a dress on the 16th century tapestry 'La Dame à la Licorne'.*
(Kathleen Basford)

page 21:
Edgings
Top   Shell edge
Left   Picôt edge
Right   Crab stitch edge

3. Work one row of triple treble.
4. Join the insertion to the second piece of fabric as follows. ** remove from crochet loop, pull this loop through the embroidered chain on the other piece of fabric 1 dc in next st. Repeat from ** to end. Fasten off yarn.

Another useful idea is to substitute a pocket, yoke, or sleeve piece with crochet. A basic network of crochet can be made by working 1 tr 1 ch on each row, with all the trebles forming vertical rows. It is a versatile pattern, being small and easily shaped.

CROCHET LACE

Crochet with fine yarns will make up into pretty edgings and insertions for lingerie. Use good quality silk or cotton. If you want items to wash and wear well over a long period of time, choose a good strong durable mercerized cotton.

NARROW EDGINGS
Pattern No 1 (Narrow Edging)

a. Coats Mercer Crochet No 60 Hook 0.75
b. Coats Mercer Crochet No 10 Hook 1.75
Commence with 12 ch.
Row 1. 1 tr into the 6th ch from the hook 3 ch, miss 2 ch (of foundation ch), 1 tr into 9th ch, 2 ch, miss 2 ch, 1 tr into 12th ch; turn.
Row 2. 6 ch, 1 dtr into the middle space (of 3 ch), *2ch and 1 dtr in same place, rep from * twice (there should be 4 dtr in the same place), then 1 dtr into the 2nd (of 5 ch) of last row; turn.
Row 3. 5 ch, 1 dtr in middle space (of 2 ch of last row), 3 times work 2 ch and 1 dtr in same space (4 dtr in all); 1 dtr into loop of 6 ch of previous row, and into same loop work 2 ch and 1 dtr 5 times (making 6 dtr); 1 dtr in the 12th ch of foundation ch; turn.
Row 4. 5 ch and 1 dc in each of the spaces of 2 ch, 5 ch, 1 dtr in middle space of 3rd row, 3 times work 2 ch and 1 dtr in same space, 1 dtr on 2nd ch at end of row; turn.

Row 5. 5 ch, 1 dtr in middle space of 4th row, 3 times work 2 ch and 1 dtr in same space, 1 dtr on 4th dtr (of 4th row); turn.

Repeat from 2nd row, only in the 3rd row of each succeeding scallop, after the 6th dtr, the last dtr is worked into the 4th dtr stitch of 4th row.

Pattern No 2 (Narrow Edging)

a. Coats Mercer Crochet No 40 Hook 0.75
b. Twilleys Twenty   Hook 1.25
Commence with 16 chain
Row 1. Use 5 of the chain for turning; 1 tr into the 6th ch *3 ch, 1 tr, rep twice more from * into the same hole, 6 ch, miss 5 ch, 1 tr into next ch, miss 3 ch, 1 tr.

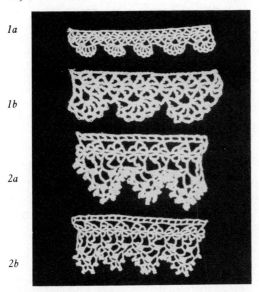

1a

1b

2a

2b

Samples of narrow edgings.

Row 2. 5 ch, 3 tr into the first hole after turning, 6 ch, miss next hole of 6 ch of previous row, 1 tr into the centre loop of 3 ch *3 ch, 1 tr*, rep twice into the same hole.

Row 3. 5 ch 1 tr into the centre loop of 3 ch of previous row, *3 ch, 1 tr into same place, rep from * twice more, 4 ch, 1 tr into the centre of the 6 ch of previous row, 3 ch 1 tr into the same place, 4 ch, 1 tr into 5 ch loop, 3 ch, 1 tr into same hole.
Row 4. 5 ch, 3 tr into the 1st hole, 5 ch, miss the next hole, 3 tr into the hole made by 3 ch, 4 ch, 1 tr into centre loop of 3 ch of last row, *3 ch, 1 tr into same place; rep from * twice more.
1st row of 2nd point: 5 ch, 1 tr into the centre loop of 3 ch, *3 ch, 1 tr into same place, * rep twice more, 6 ch, 1 tr into 1st hole of 4 ch, 3 ch, 1 tr into the same place, rep from 3rd row.
Inside edge 7 ch and 2 dc into each hole 2nd row 1 tr, *2 ch, miss 2 ch, 1 tr into next chain.
Outside edge Join cotton into work: 1 tr into same hole, *6 ch, 1 dc back into the fifth chain to form picot; 1 ch, 1 tr, rep from * into each hole (having 3 picots on each side of the point and 2 picots in the top of point)
NB. When a tr starts a row, substitute 3 ch.

page 24 left:
Deep edging *in crochet lace. Worked in crochet thread no.20, hook 1.25. The outer row of flowers is worked first. The inner flower pattern is worked separately, then the two are linked by double chain lace. Finally a line of double chain lace links the edging to the fabric (****Jennifer Rayne****).*

page 24 right:
Deep edging *in crochet lace. Chain picot and double crochet is worked to form wheels, which are linked by one picot in the last round. A chain pattern makes up the required depth to this lace (****Jennifer Rayne****).*

page 25:
Suede Waistcoat – *Each triangle of suede was first punched and then dc round. The pieces were joined in dc with small circular motifs added for a decorative effect.*
(Design Pauline Turner – worked by Louise Wheatley)

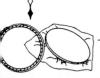

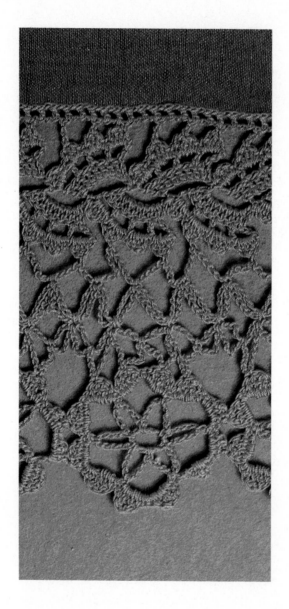

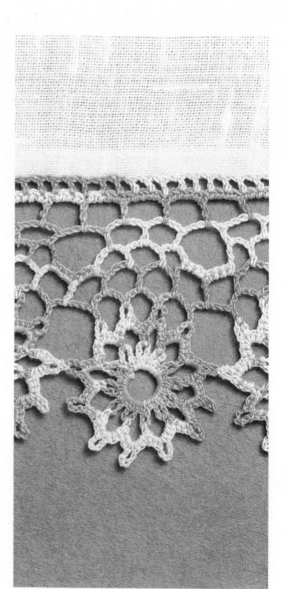

FOLLOWING A PATTERN

Some people have difficulty reading a crochet pattern. Work by the hook which takes seconds to do may need half a page of description. In order to keep the text to a reasonable length, crochet patterns employ methods and abbreviations which it is necessary to understand if the pattern is to be followed correctly.

Read instructions carefully and decide if the terms are English or American. A list of terms and abbreviations are on page 31.

How to read instructions

There is no standardisation in the way patterns are written, but in general the following rules apply:–
1. Read and act on everything placed between commas. Full stops show only the end of an abbreviation.
2. The instructions in brackets should be worked the number of times given outside the bracket *in all*.
3. When repeating from an indicated point (i.e. ★) work the number of times stated plus the original instruction.

Work a tension square

If an article is to finish the correct size it is *essential* that a tension square be worked. When following a pattern, the tension must be exact. If the crochet is only half a stitch out per 5cm square, it can end up as much as 9cm too large or too small. It is from the tension square that the correct number of stitches can be calculated for one's own design.

Work a 10cm square; measure a square of 6cm in the centre of this to obtain an exact calculation of the stitches and rows. It is vital that the tension square be used if substitute yarns are contemplated.

Joined yarn

Joined yarn should be invisible to the eye, not easily felt, and it must remain intact with washing and wearing. A general method is to work the stitch to the point where the old yarn is drawn to the front of the work. Finish the stitch with the new yarn.

Fig 19 Joining yarn

In a dense fabric simply work over the two ends at the base of the stitches. In a lacy pattern, loop the two tails through top loops of stitches to the next block (Fig 17).

Length

Length can change in wear if the yarn is heavy or the tension loose. To avoid this, pin crochet on a padded hanger between working periods allowing any drop to occur before wear.

Armhole/front and neck bands

With curved edges such as armholes and necks, patterns do not always indicate that certain points need to be increased and others decreased. It is necessary to increase on an outside curve and decrease on an inside curve. A right angle needs to gain or lose 2 stitches on the corner of every row to keep a flat mitred look. Armhole bands will have a 'frilled' look unless some stitches are lost on every row.

Fig 20 shows the best points at which to increase or decrease. Lay work flat on a smooth surface to detect buckling or pulling, and adjust stitches accordingly.

Armhole and neck shapings

If the pattern produces steps or holes at the shaping edges when you are decreasing, use the decreasing method shown in 'Basic Stitches'.

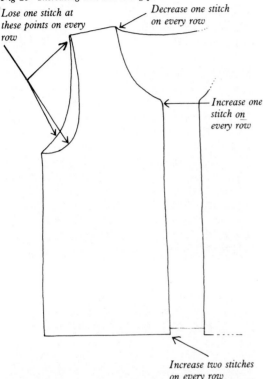

Fig 20 *Increasing and decreasing points.*

Lose one stitch at these points on every row

Decrease one stitch on every row

Increase one stitch on every row

Increase two stitches on every row

Work *1 dc in one side, 1 dc in opposite side, miss one stitch, 3 ch, repeat from * to end.

Pressing

Pressing is rarely needed and can flatten the texture, so read the ball band *before* pressing as some yarns will change under damp heat. The exceptions are fine cotton work and misshapen pieces which need pulling into shape before making up.

CREATIVE DESIGN

There are no hard and fast rules with crochet. As long as you have a loop on the hook, insert the hook into the work somewhere and draw a thread through – something will happen. If the material can be wrapped around the hook head and drawn through a loop, and if the item into which the hook is being inserted holds its form, then the range of materials to be crocheted is extended considerably. For a textured effect experiment with:-

– only working in the back loop of double crochet
– inserting the hook round the stem of trebles
– inserting the hook in stitches between stitches
– inserting the hook in stitches 2 rows below and looping the yarn up
– putting tall stitches in short stitch rows, *eg* 1 dc 1 dtr
– putting too many stitches in one row and losing them on the next

Try different materials – paper, wire, rouleau strips, binder twine etc. – as alternatives to yarn.

– work into leather, suede, sheepskin, dress/furnishing fabrics, wood, ceramics, etc.
– mix yarns of differing thicknesses and textures
– combine your favourite craft with crochet
– make one huge ball of oddments, haphazardly attaching them to each other but using no more than a quarter of a ball before changing yarn.

Making up

It is vital that *all* rows match. Most patterns advise sewing the seams together, but a back stitch may cause seams to be rigid, as will a slip stitch. Since bad joins are easily noticed in crochet because of its accentuated texture, use one of the following methods:
1. Double – crochet the seams by placing right sides of work together and inserting the hook through both pieces. This allows a slight movement during laundering as well as enclosing any unsightly edges and ends of yarn.
2. If work is lacy use a 'faggot' type join as follows:-

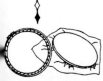

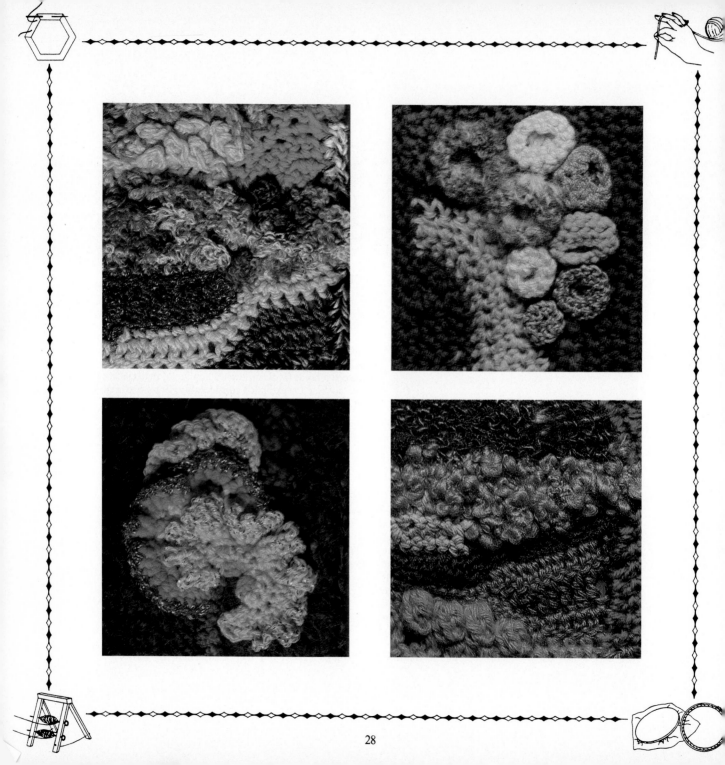

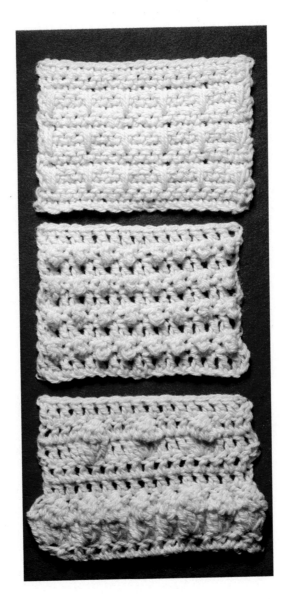

COLOUR

1. Use your selected colour in three tones – light, medium and dark – then add a little of a complementary colour chosen from the colour circle for contrast.
2. Choose colours already in the curtains, carpet or loose covers when you are making something for a room.
3. Look in magazines for colour schemes that appeal to you and take the picture with you when you buy your yarn.
4. Remember that equal amounts of tone make a colour scheme monotonous. Too many colours arranged haphazardly can be confusing, so use only one half of the colour circle at any one time. If you feel a highlight is needed, try adding a minute touch of a complementary colour.

page 28:
Creative Crochet Samples
Blue *The leaf shapes sewn on to the background are made by increasing many times into every stitch of a base row of dc*
Purple *Individual cup-shapes are sewn on to a background of double crochet*
Turquoise *The texture is achieved with the use of chain fur stitch*
Green *The texture is achieved by using popcorn stitch, and an area of bumpy yarn in a combination of double crochet and trebles* (**Jan Messent**)

page 29:
Creative Crochet Patterns
1 Trebles worked in back loop only.
2 Trebles round stem of trebles (basket st).
3 Trebles between trebles.
4 On every 4th row of dc the 3rd stitch is worked by inserting the hook two rows below.
5 One row of 1 dc, 1 dtr, between treble rows.
6 4 tr in every other st on row with 1 tr in between. Row 2 1 tr, 4 tr cluster to end 2 rows of plain treble (**Pauline Turner**)

Front cover: Creative crochet sample. (**Jan Messent**)

back cover:
Mittens *made of double knitting wool using dc, htr and tr. A rose motif is added on the backs. The ties are spirals made with 9 ch and working 8 trebles in each ch.*
(**Kathleen Basford**)

HOOK SIZES

English Wool	English Cotton	Standard International	American Wool	American Cotton
	7½			
	7	0.60		14
	6½	0.75		13
	6	–		12
	5½	1.00		11
	5	–		10
	4½	1.25		9
	4	–		8
16	3½	1.50		7
	3			
15	2½	1.75		6
	2	–	A	5
14	1½	2.00	B	4
		–		3
13	1	–	C	2
12	0	2.50	D	1
11	2/0	–	E	0
10	3/0	3.00	F	2/0
9		3.50	G	
8		4.00	H	
7		4.50	I	
6		5.00	J	
5		5.50		
4		6.00		–
3		–		
2		7.00	K	
0		8.00		
000		9.00		
		10.00		
		12.00		
		15.00		
		16.00		

ABBREVIATIONS

	English	American
alternate	alt	
approximately	approx	
beginning	beg	
block(s)	blk(s)	
centimetre(s)	cm(s)	
chain	ch	ch
cluster	cl	
continue	cont	
contrast	C	
crab stitch	crst.	
decreasing	dec	
double crochet	dc	single crochet (sc)
double treble	dtr	treble (tr)
group(s)	gr(s)	
half treble	htr	half double crochet (hdc)
inch(es)	in(s)	
increasing	inc	
loop(s)	lp(s)	
main colour	'm'	
millimetre	mm	
pattern(s)	patt(s)	
picot	p	
puff stitch	pst	
quadruple treble	quadtr	triple treble (triptr)
remain	rem	
repeat	rep	
right side	RS	
shell	sh	
slip stitch	ss	slst
space(s)	sp(s)	
stitch(es)	st(s)	
treble	tr	double crochet (dc)
triple treble	triptr	double treble (dtr)
together	tog	
wrong side	WS	
yarn round hook	yrh	

Any special stitches used to produce a particular texture are usually fully described in the pattern with the appropriate abbreviation.

SYMBOLS

Stitches

+ or •	double crochet
	half treble
	treble
	double treble
	triple treble
	quadruple treble

Links

	chain
∩ or	slip stitch
	loop
	picot

Groups

	block (of trebles)
	group (of trebles)
	cluster (of trebles)
	puff stitch (using trebles)
	increase

inside front cover:
Paddle Design
Commence with 9 ch join with a ss to form a ring
Row 1 Into ring work 16 dc, ss into first dc.
Row 2 1 dc into same place as ss *5 ch miss 1 dc, 1 dc into
next dc rep from *ending with 5 ch, 1 ss into first dc.
Row 3 1 dc into same place as ss, *2 dc into next 5 ch sp, 4
ch, 1 dc into next dc, rep from * ending with 1 ss into first dc.
4th to 15th Row
*1 dc into next dc and into each remaining dc of dc group, 2
dc into 4 ch sp, 4 ch, miss first dc of next dc group: rep from *
all round (15 dc into each dc group on last row).
Row 16 *1 dc into each of next 13 dc, 4 ch, 1 dc into next 4
ch sp, 4 ch, miss next dc; rep from * all round.
Row 17 *1 dc into each of next 11 dc, (5 ch, 1 dc into next
loop) twice, 5 ch, miss next dc, rep from * all round.
Continue in this manner, having 2 dc less in each dc group
and 1 loop more between dc groups on each row until 1 dc
remains in each dc group, ending with 1 ch, 1 tr into first dc.

Acknowledgments
Series editor: Kit Pyman

Text by Pauline Turner. Drawings by Jan Messent.
Photographs by Search Press Studios

Text, illustrations, arrangement and typography copyright
© Search Press Limited 1983.

Reprinted 1985, 1986, 1989

First published in Great Britain in 1983 by Search Press
Limited, Wellwood, North Farm Road, Tunbridge Wells,
Kent TN2 3DR.

ISBN 0 85532 451 1

Made and printed in Spain by A. G. Elkar, S. Coop.
Autonomía, 71 - 48012-Bilbao - Spain